Teaching Music in the Small Church

By Marilyn J. Keiser

The Church Hymnal Corporation
800 Second Avenue, New York, New York 10017

The Church Pension Fund
800 Second Avenue
New York, N.Y. 10017

ISBN: 0-89869-102-8

Prologue

The contents of this book grow out of my work during the past twelve years as Music Consultant for the Diocese of Western North Carolina. At the invitation of local priests and musicians, I have visited the parishes and missions of the Diocese, working with congregations, choirs, and organists. In the second and third chapters of this book I describe some of my visits to local congregations and the techniques I have used for teaching new music and helping congregations and choirs participate in singing the liturgy.

In all of my work I owe an enormous debt of gratitude to the Rev. Alex Viola for his help in setting up the Music Consultant position in this Diocese in 1970, to the Rt. Rev. George M. Henry, the Bishop who hired me, and to our present Bishop, the Rt. Rev. William G. Weinhauer. I would like to acknowledge Joyce Glover for her invaluable help in the editing of this work, and I would also like to thank all of the music directors, congregations, clergy, and choirs of the Diocese of Western North Carolina whose hospitality and enthusiasm have warmed and encouraged me.

Marilyn Keiser

Chapter One

Introduction

This book grows out of my belief that music is for people. Music touches us deeply; it has the power to express feelings that we cannot put into words. As Olivier Messiaen has said, "The joy of music is that it can go beyond mere words — which are too precise. Music can express what there is in the soul."[1]

Music inspires and uplifts our worship. A congregation experiences it together — the hymns and refrains, the canticles and anthems, the psalms. This music of liturgy unifies us; it is a great corporate action.

The statements of faith, the songs of praise, the prayers of the heart are a music that we carry with us. The following story, related by Archbishop Weakland of Milwaukee, is an example:

> ...I am in Upper Volta.... One of the greatest experiences of my life happened there on Sunday morning. Everybody came from the valley up to the monastery — monasteries are always on hills — and there we had a very simple liturgy, simple instruments, simple songs. I didn't understand the dialect, but I celebrated the Mass and preached in French. After I finished my sermon, I thought the catechist was going to translate my sermon, but he started to sing.... He had put the theme of my sermon into an antiphon for them, a refrain; and they all sang it back. He sang — literally — my entire sermon, point by point. And as he sang, they put in the refrain consistently to the end. During the Communion I heard the same melody again. At the end of the Mass they all went forth singing the theme of my sermon. Then all went out and sat under trees, where the brothers instructed them. I heard them going back into the valley that night singing the refrain.[2]

Because singing is a great corporate action binding congregations together, the teaching of music and the encouragement of singing have been important emphases of my work as Music Consultant for the Diocese of Western North Carolina during the past twelve years. This work has taken me to congregational hymn-sings in this diocese and beyond. I have met with music directors, clergy groups, and choirs. Some of my visits to congregations and choirs have been designed to teach new hymns, canticles, or music for the Eucharist; other visits have been arranged purely for the purpose of bringing people of all ages together to sing.

Local Diversity

The religious texture of our society includes many strands; in visiting local congregations I have found great diversity. Just as these congregations are distinctive, so are the musical sounds in their worship. The mosaic of dulcimers, guitars, flutes, and motet choirs are part of our local color and diversity.

> ...The steel band in the Caribbean and the drums in Africa are very different from the harmonium in an Indian village and from the magnificent organ in Westminster Abbey. The...sounds made by these instruments and the voices which the instruments accompany are of great variety. Yet all have the same object — to proclaim the glory of the very same God.[3]

We may acknowledge this diversity of musical sounds and religious strands, but how do we come to realize a music that will enrich and enhance the liturgical life of a worshiping community?

David Babin has written, "...for a liturgy to be real, it must be honest. In other words, if it is to be an authentic symbol, it must reflect life as it actually is."[4] In the same way, music of the liturgy must be an honest expression of each individual worshiping community. For a small church to attempt to imitate the music program at a large church would be unnatural. An authentic music emerges out of the resources of each congregation.

What are the local resources, and how can they be developed? These are key questions. A music which will enliven and enrich the liturgical life of a worshiping congregation has no blueprint. That which is appropriate will vary from place to place. Often the most effective sounds are the simplest ones — plainsong, a single flute, a unison anthem, a quiet dulcimer.

We Are All Artists

The musicians who offer these sounds — the amateur organists, the professional church musicians, the motet singers, the African drummers, the dulcimer players — are all artists. Erik Routley has said: "Art, being one of the manifestations of the Holy Spirit's work in the world, is a dimension of life — every man is an artist, a self-giver, a self-revealer, if he is allowed to be."[5]

- We are all artists.
- For each worshiping community there is *a music*.
- Simple sounds are often the most effective ones.
- Music is for people.

These are some of the themes of this book.

Chapter Two

Working with Congregations

> I would not care to be sure, but my guess is that the
> real growing point of modern church music is
> congregational music.... I am not in the least anxious
> about the cathedral settings and anthems and cantatas
> of the future, but I do still wonder who is going to
> compose today's DOWN AMPNEY. Who will produce
> what to this generation is quite new and
> contemporary, and what in the year 1995 we shall
> have to choose with care because popularity has led to
> its over-use? Who will meet the congregation where it
> is and lead it, at its own pace, a step or two forward
> on its own road? That's the really grass-root question.
> My guess at its answer is that it will be somebody
> who knows as much about people as about music,
> and a great deal about both.[1]

Erik Routley's guess that "...the real growing point of modern church
music is congregational music..."[2] would seem accurate in light of the
emphasis on congregational participation found in the *Book of
Common Prayer* and in revised services of other denominations as well.
Modern composers have responded by writing psalm settings, canticles,
and music for the Eucharist which involve the congregation in singing
simple refrains and antiphons. Recent hymnals and supplements include
hymn tunes that are readily accessible to congregations.

The enrichment of the musical life of congregations has been one of the
primary emphases of my work as a Music Consultant in the Diocese of
Western North Carolina. Here the majority of churches are small.
Clergy who serve these churches ask, "What is possible with limited
musical resources? How can we encourage the congregation to sing
out?"

The participation of any congregation will depend in large measure on the music we choose. Music irradiates words. Set a glorious text to a dull tune and the hymn will never become vibrantly alive. The careful wedding of a great text and tune like "Come down, O Love divine" to DOWN AMPNEY, and "A mighty fortress is our God" to EIN' FESTE BURG, can create a thrilling and inspiring experience of worship. Dr. Routley describes the feeling of a congregation singing Samuel Johnson's "City of God":

> The writer uses poetry as much as he can; the
> musician adds music...and the result is something that
> goes right to the heart of the congregation, and comes
> out not as Samuel Johnson being sung by a group of
> Christians, but as a group of Christians singing its
> belief.[3]

Congregational Hymn-Sings

With enthusiastic leadership, music in the smallest church can be spirited. Congregational hymn-sings are an effective way of strengthening and enlivening the people's participation. They also provide an opportunity for music leaders to teach new hymns.

In working with diocesan congregations, I have found that weeknights or Sunday nights are effective times to teach new hymns and service music. (Sunday morning congregational rehearsals are sometimes viewed as an intrusion to worship.) Also, the informal setting of a parish hall frees people to make comments and ask questions and establishes a bond of unity among different age groups.

The process of teaching new music on such occasions should be kept as simple as possible. I often begin with familiar hymns—ones which both children and adults will know. Then I teach several new pieces but not so many that the people are overwhelmed. The presence of choir members (who may already have learned the music) gives a lift to the singing. I sometimes ask the children to sing a verse of a hymn alone, or I ask the women and girls, or everyone with blond hair. I enjoy closing an evening by asking the people to choose their favorite hymns.

10

If possible, prior to the hymn-sing I work with a small group of singers who then can serve as teachers for the rest of the congregation. Using such a small group works well in teaching hymns like "Jesu, Jesu, fill us with your love" and "Lift high the cross." Both of these hymns begin with refrains which the congregation can learn immediately.

Hymns III, H-213
Tom Colvin

Je - su, Je - su, fill us with your love, show

us how to serve the neigh-bors we have from you.

Hymns III, H-125
Sidney H. Nicholson

Lift high the cross, the

love of Christ pro - claim till all the world

a - dore his sa - cred **Name.**

In teaching these hymns, the verses may be sung by the choir or a small group of singers—children or adults.

Hymns III, H-213
Tom Colvin

Verse

1 Kneels at the feet of his friends, si-lent-ly wash-es their
2 Neigh-bors are rich and poor, neigh-bors are black and
3 These are the ones we should serve, these are the ones we should
4 Lov-ing puts us on our knees, serv-ing as though we were

feet, mas-ter who acts as a slave to them.
white, neigh-bors are near-by and far a - way.
love. All are neigh-bors to us and you.
slaves; this is the way we should live with you.

Hymns III, H-125
Sidney H. Nicholson

1 Come, let us fol - low where our Cap-tain trod, our
2 Led on their way by this tri - um-phant sign, the
3 Each new-born ser - vant of the Cru-ci - fied bears
4 O Lord, once lift - ed on the glo-rious tree, as
5 So shall our song of tri - umph ev - er be: praise

Repeat Refrain

1 King vic - to - rious, Christ the Son of God. Org.
2 hosts of God in con-qu'ring ranks com-bine.
3 on the brow the seal of him who died.
4 thou hast prom - ised, draw the world to thee.
5 to the Cru - ci - fied for vic - to - ry.

12

In the first of three visits to one of our diocesan churches, the Church of the Transfiguration in Bat Cave, I met with six or seven singers prior to dinner. I rehearsed the Communion Service of Healey Willan as well as several hew hymns. After dinner, I worked with members of the congregation.

We began the evening by singing several familiar hymns, then started to work on the three-fold *Kyrie* of Healey Willan. I asked the small group that I had worked with before dinner to sing it through; then everyone sang. Finally, I talked about some of the melodic and rhythmic elements in the *Kyrie*. The presentation went like this:

> Good. Notice the way the composer repeats the rhythm in the first two phrases:

> The melodies of those first two phrases are very similar.

> The last phrase is extended. This time Healey Willan sets three notes to the word "Lord."

> Now let's sing it all the way through.

On my visits to small congregations I find it best to sing through a new piece before discussing the musical elements; that way, the people experience the flow of the entire piece. I also find it helpful to stand close to the people, snapping my fingers to keep the rhythm alive on a long note, tapping the top of the closest pew, or conducting in a traditional pattern. When children are present, I ask them to sing a phrase by themselves, sometimes clapping, tapping, or counting on their fingers so that they can feel the forward motion of the rhythm.

At the Church of the Transfiguration, as we began work on the Willan *Sanctus*, I again asked the small group of singers to sing for the rest of the congregation. After everyone sang the *Sanctus*, I talked about the musical climax that occurs on the word "Glory."

> Notice how the composer sustains the highest note.
> Sing into the word "Glory." Feel an accent on the first
> beat of the new measure — "Glo – o." The rest of the
> phrase relaxes from the top note.

The whole musical line leads up to that high note. Healey Willan builds a natural crescendo into the phrase. I think that it would be impossible to sing that "Glory" softly.

Hymnal 1940, 711
Healey Willan

The presence of children often provides an opportunity for simple, direct comments which speak to adults as well. I often talk to children about composers or hymn texts and tunes, or I ask them questions about the music. In the *Sanctus*, I might ask:

> I mentioned a feeling of natural crescendo in Healey Willan's *Sanctus*. Could one of you tell me what "crescendo" means?

> Is it like the sound of an approaching train? Does it mean that we sing faster, too? No? What word is used in music to tell you to sing faster?

Much of my work with small congregations and the musicians who serve them has been to explore further the resources of *The Hymnal* and its supplements. On one such visit, we began with "Joyful, joyful, we adore thee" and talked about the Beethoven tune, HYMN TO JOY. We

15

sang several other hymns of praise and talked about the tunes wed to those texts. Then we looked at unfamiliar texts like St. Francis of Assisi's "Most High, omnipotent, good Lord" and Christopher Smart's "We sing of God the mighty source." Finally, we looked at a new hymn tune, DE TAR, which may be sung to several familiar texts, including "O Master, let me walk with thee," "O love, how deep, how broad, how high," and "O love of God, how strong and true." The composer of DE TAR, Calvin Hampton, has pointed out that in his experience, "...singing familiar words to a tune not normally associated with them has the effect of jarring one into being attentive to their meaning."[4]

I introduced DE TAR using the text, "O love of God, how strong and true." The tune is step-wise and has melodic repetition. I played the melody alone the first time through, adding the accompaniment and obbligato later.

Hymns III, H-224
Calvin Hampton

Notice the melodic repetition in phrases 1 and 3 and again in 2 and 4. In the first and third phrases, each syllable is sung to an eighth note. (I played and sang those two lines.) Now listen to phrases 2 and 4 — the syllables move at half the pace. For me, it makes a very satisfying balance.

During a week-long tour through the Diocese of Texas several years ago, I spent a great deal of time with congregations and choirs, clergy and music directors. On several occasions I introduced service music for Rite II, beginning like this:

Let's sing through Robert Powell's setting of the *Sanctus*. There is a natural flow of ideas in this setting; phrases begin with the same melodic patterns; the rhythm is not difficult. You might find it helpful to teach this to your congregation a phrase at a time like this:

Ho - ly, ho - ly, ho - ly— Lord, God of pow-er and might,

Notice that each of the three "Holys" begins with the same two notes. I'll sing it one more time, then we'll all sing.

The next phrase introduces a triplet figure which is used twice — on "heaven" and "full of."

heav-en and earth are full of your glo - ry,

Finally, the highest note, on "Hosanna."

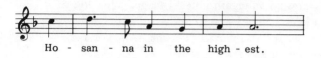

Ho - san - na in the high - est.

The *Benedictus* begins with the triplet figure you just
sang and ends with the same "Hosanna."

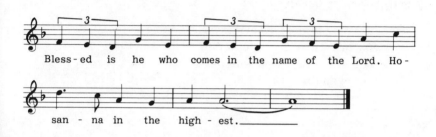

Bless - ed is he who comes in the name of the Lord. Ho -
san - na in the high - est._____

Church Hymnal Series One, Setting One
Robert Powell

Ho - ly, ho - ly, ho - ly__ Lord, God of pow-er and
might, heav-en and earth are full of your glo - ry, Ho -
san - na in the high - est. Bless - ed is he who
comes in the name of the Lord. Ho - san-na in the high-est.____

On a visit to another congregation, we worked on a new *Te Deum* set to Anglican chant. I talked about the style and flow of the new pointing with fewer syllables on the reciting note (see the *Book of Canticles*), and I mentioned the use of brackets over syllables or words which are to be sung to one note of the chant (for example: brightness, they will).

We began by reading the text aloud.

> All the stresses should be those of good reading. Now sing the text on one pitch. Work for a smooth flow, giving slight emphasis to the important syllables.
>
> Watch the three- and four-syllable words: "everlasting," "majesty," "eternal," "glorious."
>
> Good. Now I'll play the chant tune one more time and we'll sing it all the way through.

I was invited by the rector of a small church in Canton, North Carolina, to teach new hymns and service music to his congregation on three successive Wednesday nights during Lent. On each occasion we worked in the parish hall where a piano could be moved close to the people. Each week we sang several new pieces, reviewed music learned the previous week, and ended with familiar hymns. The value of successive visits was immeasurable. Everyone seemed genuinely enthusiastic about the new music, and the weekly repetition gave them an opportunity to learn the music well and feel comfortable with it.

The first week, I introduced a new tune to George Herbert's text, "Let all the world in every corner sing."

> I'll play the tune through on the piano. Notice the similarity of the melody in the first and second phrases.

(1)

1 Let all the world in ev - 'ry cor - ner

sing, My God and King!

(2)

Let all the world in ev - 'ry cor - ner

sing, My God and King!

Now the melody takes a new turn...and the final phrase is a reiteration of the opening melody. We'll sing it in unison. I'll play the accompaniment in a minute.

(3)

The heav'ns are not too high, His praise may thith - er

(4)

fly: The earth is not too low, His

praises there may grow. Let

all the world in ev - 'ry cor - ner sing, My

God and King!

The tune has innate singability — there is a repetition and the melody flows naturally from phrase to phrase. The congregation learned it quickly. We sang stanza two as the composer suggested — men singing phrase one, women phrase two, and everyone in unison on the succeeding phrases.

Hymnal Supplement II, 770
Calvin Hampton

MacDougall

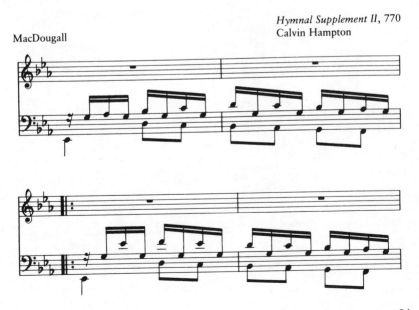

1 Let ... all the world in ev - 'ry cor - ner
2 Let ... all the world in ev - 'ry cor - ner

sing, My God and King!
sing, My God and King!

Women

Let all the world in ev - 'ry cor - ner
Let all the world in ev - 'ry cor - ner

sing, My God and King! The
sing, My God and King! The

Full

22

heav'ns are not too high, His praise may thith-er
Church with psalms must shout, No door can keep them

fly: The earth is not too low, His
out: But, a - bove all, the heart

prais - es there may grow. Let
bear the long - est part. Let

all the world in ev - 'ry cor - ner sing, My
all the world in ev - 'ry cor - ner sing, My

23

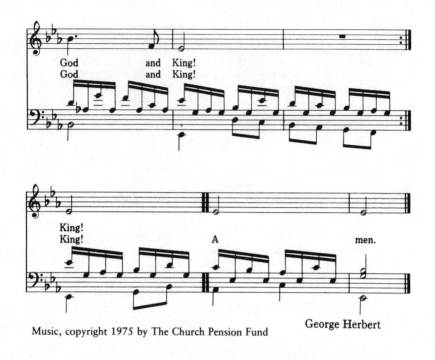

God   and King!
God   and King!

King!
King!   A   men.

George Herbert

Following "Let all the world" we sang through Rite II service music and ended the evening with familiar hymns of their choosing.

On many of my diocesan visits to congregations, retirement communities, junior choirs, and women's groups, I carry a set of handbells. The bells enliven singing and provide another way of involving people of all ages. On one December visit to Brasstown, we ended the evening singing favorite Christmas carols. When "Angels we have heard on high" was chosen, I handed out bells for the chord of F Major. The bell players stood close to the piano.

> When I nod my head, play your bells. Let's try the bells alone once.

> Good. Now with the carol...(Asterisks indicate where the people ring the bells.)

Hymnal 1940, 42
French Carol Melody
arr. by Edward Shippen Barnes

GLORIA

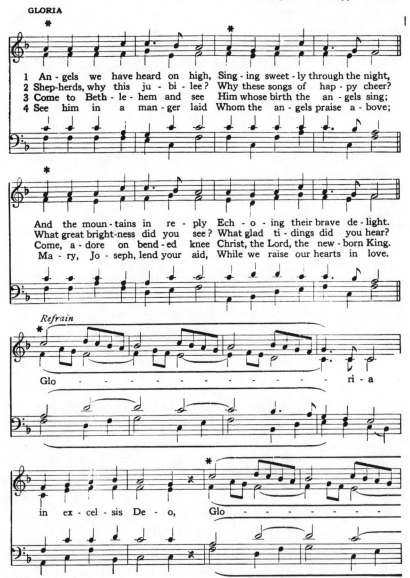

1 An-gels we have heard on high, Sing-ing sweet-ly through the night,
2 Shep-herds, why this ju-bi-lee? Why these songs of hap-py cheer?
3 Come to Beth-le-hem and see Him whose birth the an-gels sing;
4 See him in a man-ger laid Whom the an-gels praise a-bove;

And the moun-tains in re-ply Ech-o-ing their brave de-light.
What great bright-ness did you see? What glad ti-dings did you hear?
Come, a-dore on bend-ed knee Christ, the Lord, the new-born King.
Ma-ry, Jo-seph, lend your aid, While we raise our hearts in love.

Refrain

Glo - - - - - - - - - - - - - ri - a

in ex-cel-sis De - o, Glo - - - - - - ri - a

25

Traditional French Carol, alt. by EARL MARLATT, 1937

We used the bells on other carols — "O come, all ye faithful," and "O come, O come, Emmanuel."

At the Church of the Incarnation in Highlands, we used bells to accompany the Ghana folk song, "Jesu, Jesu, fill us with your love." This time, I divided those who wanted to play bells into three groups. I assured them no experience was required.

> Let's put the people in Group I on my left, Group II in front of me, and Group III to my right. I'll point at each group when it is your time to play. (The people in Group I play the chord of E Major; those in Group II play F# Minor; and those in Group III play the chord of B Major.)

Hymns III, H-213
Tom Colvin

Verse

(I)

1	Kneels	at	the	feet	of	his	friends,		si - lent - ly	wash - es their
2	Neigh-bors	are	rich		and		poor,		neigh-bors are	black and
3	These	are	the	ones	we	should	serve,		these are	the ones we should
4	Lov - ing	puts	us	on	our	knees,			serv - ing	as though we were

feet,	mas -ter who acts as a	slave	to	them.
white,	neigh-bors are near-by and	far	a -	way.
love.	All are neigh-bors to	us	and	you.
slaves;	this is the way we should	live	with	you.

In recent visits to diocesan churches, I have explored the resources of *Hymns III*, pointing out the format of the pages, the special indices, and the lectionary references in the Table of Contents. I have begun these sessions with familiar tunes — TALLIS' CANON ("O gracious light"); DARWALL'S 148TH ("To God with gladness sing"); or LASST UNS ERFREUN ("All creatures of our God and King").

At each of these sessions we have talked about the use of metrical canticles and psalms and have sung examples of each, e.g.,

> Come, let us join our cheerful songs (A Song to the
>   Lamb, *Dignus es*)
> Tell out, my soul (The Song of Mary, *Magnificat*)
> To God with gladness sing (*Venite*)
> My Shepherd will supply my need (Psalm 23)
> God of mercy, God of grace (Psalm 67)
> New songs of celebration render (Psalm 98)

We have read and sung Baptism and Eucharistic hymns; for example: the Stanford tune, ENGELBERG, to "We know that Christ is raised and dies no more;" Leo Sowerby's beautiful tune, ROSEDALE, to "Come, risen Lord, and deign to be our guest;" and the American folk melody, LAND OF REST, to "I come with joy to meet my Lord."

At one session in Hickory, we sang hymns appropriate to Holy Week, beginning with "Lift high the cross" and continuing with such hymns as "My song is love unknown," "Jesu, Jesu, fill us with your love," and "Through the Red Sea brought at last." Before we sang "Through the Red Sea," one of the hymns appropriate to the Easter Vigil, I played the tune through and talked about it as I played, pointing out the melodic repetition in the first two lines, the repeated use of Alleluia, and the short phrases in the third line. The first time they sang, I played only the melody line, adding the harmony for the second and third stanzas.

In working with all of these small congregations, I have focused on the sweep and power of new music and also on making that music accessible, whether by playing the melody alone, teaching the music phrase by phrase, or pointing out the repetition of a rhythmic or melodic line. When it has been appropriate, I have also drawn on local resources — a recorder group, a fine soloist, a small group of singers, a quiet flute, or a high school pianist playing an obbligato.

The following techniques have proven effective in my work:

- beginning with familiar hymns
- teaching a few new pieces but not so many as to overwhelm
- interspersing new materials with familiar tunes that people can sing easily
- rehearsing in an informal setting, with a piano moved close to the people
- incorporating a large measure of variety and spontaneity
- maintaining a balance of the familiar and the new

Summary

Clearly, the *Book of Common Prayer* provides many opportunities for new and enriching experiences. The flexible framework of the Prayer

Book services invites new sounds and fresh approaches to the use of the arts in worship. The growing emphasis on lay participation and congregational *in*clusion necessitates clear, thoughtful consideration in choosing music of worship.

Significant new hymns have emerged. In teaching these hymns and other service music to congregations, careful planning and cooperation among clergy, choir director, and instrumentalists are vital. A new canon on church music, passed by the 1976 General Convention, stresses the need for joint responsibility on the part of clergy and musicians in determining what music is "appropriate to the context in which it is used."[5] Erik Routley has noted: "Too often...each major participant in worship plays a solo without reference to anybody else.... All of which is very much to the detriment of public worship, or, at all events, it means that opportunities are being lost."[6]

In all planning of liturgy, in teaching new service music and hymns, we — musicians and clergy — must work closely together, choosing music that will lead a congregation "...at its own pace, a step or two forward on its own road."[7] In incorporating this new music, we must stay attuned to the pastoral needs of our congregations. We must prepare ourselves with the utmost care, respond with patience as well as eagerness, and communicate the essence of music as sung prayer.

Chapter Three

Working with Choirs

Choirs of children and adults have important roles in leading and teaching. They lead congregational song and spoken responses and lend strong support to the teaching of new hymns, refrains, and antiphons. Their own special offerings may be hymn settings, anthems, motets, canticles, or psalms.

Many small churches have no choir; in some places, a group of singers may meet only to prepare an anthem for a festival service, a patronal feast, or the bishop's annual visit. Other churches would like to have an active music program but lack the funds to buy choral music or pay a trained organist. Many need help in locating music accessible to a small choir.

The following letters, written soon after I began my work as a diocesan Music Consultant, illustrate some of these problems:

> I need help. I am so in need of music for the choir. Can you send me the name and address of a church which might be cleaning out their file.... Also, is there a music store where I could go and look over the music myself?[1]

> We wonder if you could suggest an anthem for our choir to sing at Easter. We have a new soprano with quite a good voice and some experience in choirs. She has sung a number of solos. If you have something we could borrow, twelve copies would be enough....[2]

Choirs are often tempted to sing music beyond their capabilities. Important resources for small choirs of any denomination are a hymnal and the Psalter. *The Hymnal* and its supplements provide a great variety of simple, appropriate anthems. Resources like *Hymns III*, *Ecumenical Praise*, and *Westminster Praise* offer a wealth of material.

Psalm settings like Malcolm Williamson's *Carols of King David* are interesting and accessible.

The Hymnal as a Resource

The Standing Commission on Church Music has found that the average Episcopal parish uses only 100 to 150 of the 600 hymns in *The Hymnal*. Many of the less familiar hymns are appropriate anthems for small choirs. Plainsong hymns like "O come, Creator Spirit, come" (VENI CREATOR), "Sing, my tongue, the glorious battle" (PANGE LINGUA), and "Humbly I adore thee" (ADORO DEVOTE), which are often difficult for a congregation, may be sung by the choir. Hymns like "Come with us, O blessèd Jesus," "Deck thyself, my soul, with gladness," "All my hope on God is founded," or "Holy Spirit, ever living" may be sung by the choir at the offertory or during the communion of the people.

Working with several choirs at a workshop, I discussed ways of introducing and using these hymns:

> "Deck thyself, my soul, with gladness" might be sung a number of ways: one stanza in parts, another by the men or women, a third in unison. The children might sing one stanza or the organist could play a chorale prelude on its tune, SCHMÜCKE DICH, as the introduction to the first stanza.

> ADORO DEVOTE could be sung alternating high and low voices — men on stanzas one and three; women on stanzas two and four.

> Another beautiful hymn is "Most High, omnipotent, good Lord." This text was written by St. Francis of Assisi. Stanzas one and eight might be sung in unison with groups of men, women, and children singing alternate stanzas.

The Christmas hymn, "On this day, earth shall ring," is set in *Hymns III* to a wonderful tune by Gustav Holst. You might use handbells or tubular bells on the descending scale in the accompaniment.

Hymns III, H-113a
harm. Gustav Holst

"Eternal Ruler of the ceaseless round" might be sung alternately in unison or in parts. The tune and text are both very strong. This tune was written by Orlando Gibbons in 1623.

The text of John Donne's poem, "Wilt thou forgive that sin," is from the same period in history — 1633. This is a powerful text which is set to two tunes in *Hymns III*. Both are excellent Lenten anthems.

Hymns and hymn-anthems may be varied by the occasional addition of instruments — flutes, violins, trumpets, handbells. Bells are especially effective in accompanying plainsong hymns and canticles. (See Proulx, Richard: *Tintinnabulum*.)[3]

Familiar hymn texts sung to new tunes may also be used as anthems. (See Appendix I.) For example, "Come, risen Lord, and deign to be our guest" sung to ROSEDALE or "Father, we thank thee who hast planted" sung to ALBRIGHT are appropriate communion or offertory anthems. Calvin Hampton's tune, DE TAR, may be sung to "O Love, how deep, how broad, how high" or to "O Love of God, how strong and true." (See Chapter Two.) Settings of familiar carol texts like Malcolm Williamson's *Six Christmas Songs* are very interesting and especially appropriate for children's choirs. These six songs are written in the popular style of much of Williamson's "public music."

I introduced one of the songs, "Angels, from the Realms of Glory," at a choir workshop:

> Listen to the way Malcolm Williamson takes the
> melody and rhythm of the opening phrase and
> develops it in the next three phrases.

An - gels, from the realms of glo - ry,____

Wing your flight o'er all the earth;____

Ye who sang cre - a - tion's sto - ry,____

Now pro-claim Mes - si - ah's birth:____

The accompaniment is a series of open fifths. I like
the fresh, uncluttered sound.

Now Williamson takes the melody in a new direction
on "Come and worship." The accompaniment
changes, too — the chords are more complete and the
harmony drives to the end of the phrase.

Come_ and_ wor - ship,

On the final note, on the word "King," Williamson
returns to the open fifths in the accompaniment. It's a
magical moment.

Wor-ship Christ,_ the new-born King.

On occasion, hymns or German chorale tunes may be sung by the choir as an introduction or response to an organ prelude on the same melody. For example, the choir's singing of "Jesus, all my gladness" might be introduced by one of Johann Walther's variations on JESU, MEINE FREUDE or by J. S. Bach's setting of that chorale in the *Orgelbüchlein*. "Blessèd Jesus, at thy word" might be sung following an organ setting of LIEBSTER JESU.

The Choir as Teacher

Choirs assume an important role in teaching new hymns, canticles, and service music to congregations. Their presence adds strong support to Sunday morning, weeknight, or Sunday night rehearsals, whichever is most effective in a local parish.

At a number of diocesan churches, I met with choirs to teach canticles and hymns which later would be taught to their congregations. In working on new canticle texts, I suggested they not use Anglican chant tunes already familiar to the congregation. It would be easier for the people to learn new tunes to such new texts as The Third Song of Isaiah (*Surge, illuminare*), The Song of the Redeemed (*Magna et mirabilia*), The Song of Mary (*Magnificat*), or the *Jubilate Deo* in Rite II Morning Prayer. (Musical settings for all of these appear in the *Book of Canticles*.)

We sang several plainsong canticles, and I discussed the use of these settings with antiphons. These short, simple melodies can be taught easily to the congregation.

Book of Canticles, C-36

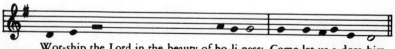

Wor-ship the Lord in the beauty of ho-li-ness: Come let us a-dore him.

I also talked about the notation of these antiphons and plainsong tones:

> The emphasis on congregational participation — music
> for the people — has meant that many recent
> publications are devoid of all unnecessary notation.
> Notice the omission of all stems on the notes. Also, in
> an attempt to smooth out the singing of unmeasured
> music, notation of the reciting notes has suggested
> pitch rather than duration. Let's look at the
> *Benedictus es, Domine.*

Book of Canticles, C-56

Tone IIIg[1]

1. Bless-ed art thou, O Lord God of our fa-thers; praised and exalted a-
bove all for ev-er. 2. Blessed art thou for the Name of thy Ma-jes-ty;
praised and exalted a-bove all for ev-er. 3. Blessed art thou in the temple
of thy ho-li-ness; praised and exalted a-bove all for ev-er.
4. Blessed art thou that beholdest the depths, and dwellest be-tween the
Che-ru-bim; praised and exalted a-bove all for ev-er. 5. Blessed art thou
on the glorious throne of thy king-dom; praised and exalted a-bove all for

ev-er. 6. Blessed art thou in the firma-ment of heav-en; praised and exalted a-

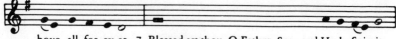

bove all for ev-er. 7. Blessed art thou, O Father, Son, and Ho-ly Spi-rit;

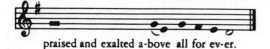

praised and exalted a-bove all for ev-er.

Chants such as this are effective with handbells. (See Appendix II.)

Psalm settings by Joseph Gelineau, Richard Proulx, and Sister Theophane Hytreck, among others, are also in this style. The congregational refrain for Gelineau's setting of Psalm 23 is short and lyrical:

Psalm 23
Joseph Gelineau

My shep-herd is the Lord, noth-ing in-deed shall I want.

Other psalm settings for unison choir and congregation include Malcolm Williamson's *Carols of King David* and twenty responsorial psalms called *Psalms of the Elements*. Among the first five of Williamson's *Carols of King David*, "I Will Lift Up Mine Eyes" incorporates a refrain that is memorable and easy to sing.

Psalm 121
Malcolm Williamson

I will lift up mine eyes un-to the hills:

Choirs of children and/or adults may sing the unison choir parts with the congregation joining in the refrain at appointed times. (A member of the choir or the choir director may signal to the congregation at the appropriate time.)

Several other psalms in these sets are immediate in their appeal: "The King of Love" (Psalm 23); "Together in Unity" (Psalm 133); "Like as the Hart" (Psalm 42); and "Lift Up Your Heads" (Psalm 24).[5] The natural flow of musical ideas in each piece is accompanied by fresh harmonies and the accompaniments are not difficult.

Many metrical psalms are appropriate anthems, e.g., "I to the hills will lift mine eyes" (Psalm 121), "Out of the depth I cry to thee" (Psalm 130), "My Shepherd will supply my need" (Psalm 23), "Let us with a gladsome mind" (Psalm 136), and "New songs of celebration render" (Psalm 98).[6]

Approaching New Music

Choir directors in small churches are faced with choosing music suitable for their choirs. What factors influence the acceptance of one anthem or hymn and the rejection of another? How does one judge the integrity of a new piece?

Daniel Moe, the conductor of the Oberlin College Choir, once commented that in looking at a new piece of music, he always tried to find a "fundamental uniqueness." In approaching a new piece of music, it is important to look for those qualities that are unique: the lyricism of the melody; the spontaneity and unpredictability of the harmony; the beauty of the composer's setting of the text; the vitality of the rhythm. Ask questions: Is the piece written in a unified idiom? Does the composer make a harmonic departure at the end of the piece (e.g., modal harmony) which has not been prepared earlier? Is there a musical climax? Is the word-setting clear? Does the music capture the spirit of the text?

In presenting anthems to small choirs, it is good to talk about some of the distinctive qualities of the music — the rhythm, the word-setting, or

an expressive melody. Several simple anthems might be introduced in
this way:

> Daniel Moe's "I Lift Up My Eyes" is an easy four-part
> setting of Psalm 121. Notice that all three verses are
> sustained and quiet. The real rhythmic interest is in
> the organ part—listen to the offbeat chords in the
> accompaniment, and the flowing quarter notes in
> verse two.[7]

"I Lift Up My Eyes"
Daniel Moe

He will not let your foot be mov'd, He'll keep you
from all harm. He who keeps Is - ra -

el,   will neith-er slum - ber___ nor   sleep.

Robert Powell's anthem "Jesus, Name of Wondrous
Love" is a two-part anthem for high and low voices.
The range is not difficult. Listen to the opening
phrase; the word-setting is very expressive.[8]

"Jesus, Name of Wondrous Love"
Robert Powell

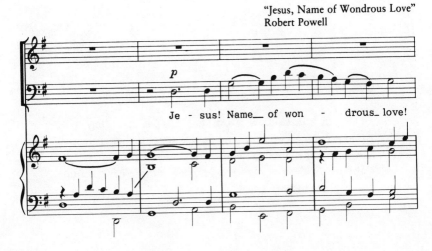

Je - sus! Name___ of won - drous_ love!

Dietrich Buxtehude's "God Shall Do My Advising" is taken from a cantata. The first stanza of this anthem is for a solo voice, a small group of singers, or children's choir. I like to add a few simple ornaments to the organ part.[9]

"God Shall Do My Advising"
Dietrich Buxtehude

43

(See Appendix III for a listing of anthems that might be helpful for small choirs.)

Nurturing Local Choirs

Combined choir festivals can be of great value in improving the music of parish churches. The present Bishop of Western North Carolina, the Rt. Rev. William G. Weinhauer, has said, "Extravaganzas are great for the morale." Singing in such festivals gives a boost to small choirs and also provides an opportunity for them to learn anthems and hymns which, in some cases, they could not sing in their local choirs. In planning festivals, however, the choice of hymns or anthems should include those which will be useful to choristers in their home parishes.

A festival might be planned around music for the Church Year; another might include many settings of psalms. The music of one composer or one country might be a theme.[10]

In preparation for one children's choir festival, I traveled to several churches to rehearse their choirs. Our theme was hymn tunes from many ages. We included a plainsong melody, Palestrina's VICTORY, a German chorale, a tune of Ralph Vaughan Williams, and others. I met with six children at the Church of the Epiphany, Newton, and we talked about several hymns:

> Let's sing "Of the Father's love begotten."

> Good. Now I want you to sing stanza one again, but we'll sing it another way — using the numbers 1, 2, 3. I'll show you. Sing the melody as smoothly as you can.

Hymnal 1940, 20
13th century Plainsong

> Do you feel the notes moving in groups of twos and threes? Now keep that same feeling and sing the words again.

Does this melody skip around or are the notes close together? I want you to compare this plainsong tune to another tune we're using at the choir festival, ST. PATRICK. Compare the first line of "I bind unto myself today" to the hymn you have just sung. In what way is it different from the plainsong tune?

St. Patrick

Hymnal 1940, 268
Traditional Irish Melody

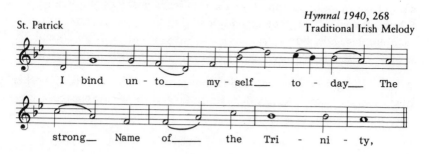

I bind un - to my - self to - day The strong Name of the Tri - ni - ty,

At St. Mark's Church, Gastonia, I taught "Come down, O Love divine."

How many of you know this hymn? Who wrote the words of this hymn? What is the name of the tune? Who was the composer of the music? When did he live? Look at the Index of Sources, Composers, and Arrangers. How many tunes by Vaughan Williams are in *The Hymnal*?

O Clap Your Hands All Ye Peoples

The future of the church's music rests in part on the musical heritage given to our young singers. The nineteenth century German educator, Friedrich Froebel (1782-1852), strongly advocated the cultivation of singing (with painting and modeling) for children, "...not with the aim of making some sort of artist out of every pupil...but with the simple and explicit intention of securing for each pupil a complete development of his nature, that he may be conscious of its wealth of interest and energy and, in particular, may be able to appreciate true art."[11]

Children in choirs receive the musical heritage of the past and present — the psalms, the liturgy. Diocesan workshops or summer camps for children extend the nurturing of young choristers. In particular, courses sponsored by a number of dioceses and the Royal School of Church Music encourage and sustain the interest of young singers by providing extra time to work on skills in singing, sight reading, and composition. They also offer special avenues for creativity in the arts.

A music camp, begun in this diocese in 1969 by the Rev. Alex Viola, emphasized singing, along with music theory and composition, handbells, eurhythmics, and Orff instruments. Near the end of one two-week music camp, a staff member and I worked with a group of children on a composition for the closing service of camp. During the two weeks, we studied unusual notation such as that in Richard Felciano's anthem, "Cosmic Festival."[12] We talked about traditional notation and the way composers communicate through a staff and a series of notes. We explored the notation of other sounds:

> How would you notate the sound of the wind? the
> dinner bell? the train? a clap of thunder?

Then we began to notate melodies that the children sang to the words "O clap your hands all ye peoples."

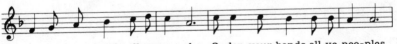
O clap your hands all ye peo-ples, O clap your hands all ye peo-ples.

The children composed rhythmic patterns, additional texts, and some interesting melodies.

Shout, shout, shout for joy, Shout, shout, shout for joy, Shout for joy!

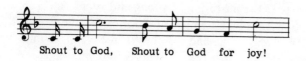

Shout to God, Shout to God for joy!

Another camper added:

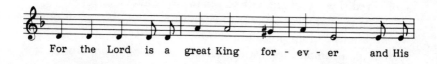

For the Lord is a great King for-ev-er and His

mer-cy rul-eth o-ver all,

Still another camper sang:

He is the King a-bove all the earth,

I think we need a concluding phrase. We always sing a *Gloria Patri* at the end of the psalms. Shall we sing a *Gloria* at the end of this, or shall we use another text?

One camper sang:

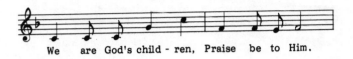

We are God's child - ren, Praise be to Him.

Another camper sang a second version:

We are God's child-ren, Praise_____ be to Him.

We asked for their ideas on a musical form for the piece. One boy suggested (∗). The star, he explained, was the explosion of the clap, the sound of the hands hitting one another, and the parentheses on either side of the star represented the hands. The campers decided to use that idea as the formal organization for the piece. The ( ) became the framework. We decided to begin and end the piece with hand clapping, using one of the rhythmic patterns the campers had composed:

The melodies were organized in a simple rondo form. The refrain, "O clap your hands all ye peoples," was used four times during the piece; each time we sang the refrain, we followed it with the clapped rhythmic pattern above. The children decided that they could provide variety by alternating the refrain with the other melodic fragments they had composed.

(Clapping)　　　　　　　　　　　O clap your hands all ye
peo-ples,　O clap your hands all ye peo-ples. (Clapping)
Shout, shout, shout for joy,　Shout, shout, shout for joy,
Shout— for joy!　Drum: tr　Shout to God, Shout to God for joy!
O clap your hands all ye peo-ples,　O clap your hands all ye
peo-ples. (Clapping)　Drum: tr　Shout to God, Shout to
God for joy!　Drum: tr　For the Lord is a great King for-
ev - er,　and His mer - cy rul - eth o - ver all.

O clap your hands all ye peo-ples, O clap your hands all ye

peo-ples. *(Clapping)* He is the King a-bove

all the earth, He is the King a-bove all the earth.

O clap your hands all ye peo-ples, O clap your hands all ye

peo-ples. *(Clapping)*

Drum:

We are God's child-ren, Praise be to Him. We are God's

child-ren, Praise_____ be to Him.

Praise_____ be to Him! *(Clapping)*

As we rehearsed for that closing service, the campers expressed their eagerness to have the entire congregation participate in their piece. They felt that while it might be difficult for everyone to learn the entire piece, the congregation could learn to clap the simple rhythmic pattern. A short rehearsal was planned before the service to teach the congregation its part. One child suggested that if members of the congregation were unsure of the rhythmic pattern after they had rehearsed it, they should just clap in their hearts.

Summary

Full, active, conscious participation is at the heart of the liturgy.[13] That full participation may be singing full voice, listening attentively, or even clapping in your heart. Fresh approaches, new ideas, careful planning, and boundless enthusiasm are vital in working with choirs of children and adults as well as in teaching congregations. Our service as musicians is to care deeply about the quality of music we choose, the integrity with which we execute it, and to keep the needs and sensitivities of the congregations we serve before us. I like John Snow's words, "Bringing music back to the human dimension, caring very much about extending rather than limiting its communication."[14]

Music is for people. "Music expresses what is in the soul."[15] St. Augustine has said that one who sings prays twice. "The first prayer is the text that is sung — a prayer to God using words; the second is the music, the singing itself, a prayer of praise from the soul."[16]

Notes

Chapter One

1 Hubert Saal quoting Olivier Messiaen, *Newsweek* 23 November 1970, p. 139.

2 Rembert Weakland, "Claim Your Art," *Pastoral Music* 5 (June-July 1981), p. 37.

3 Gerald Knight, "You in Your Small Corner," *Promoting Church Music* 4 (July 1972), p. 14.

4 David Babin, *The Celebration of Life* (New York: Morehouse-Barlow, 1969), p. 10.

5 Erik Routley, *Words, Music, and the Church* (Nashville: Abingdon Press, 1968), p. 217.

Chapter Two

1 Erik Routley, "Crossroads, Roundabout, or Last Exit to Addington?" *English Church Music 1968*, pp. 36-37.

2 Routley, "Crossroads, Roundabout," pp. 36-37.

3 Erik Routley, *Hymns Today and Tomorrow* (New York: Abingdon Press, 1964), p. 21.

4 Calvin Hampton, *Three Hymn Tunes* (Concordia Publishing House), Preface.

5 Report of the Standing Commission on Church Music to the General Convention, 1976.

6 Erik Routley, *Music Leadership in the Church* (Nashville: Abingdon Press, 1967), p. 109.

7 Routley, "Crossroads, Roundabout," p. 37.

Chapter Three

[1] From a letter of August 23, 1973.

[2] From a letter of February 15, 1973.

[3] Richard Proulx, *Tintinnabulum, The Liturgical Use of Handbells* (Chicago: G.I.A. Publications, 1980).

[4] Published by G. Schirmer.

[5] Published by Boosey and Hawkes.

[6] See listing in *Hymns III*.

[7] Published by Mercury Music Corporation.

[8] Published by Abingdon Press.

[9] Published by Concordia Publishing House.

[10] See Austin Lovelace's *Hymn Festivals,* The Papers of the Hymn Society of America, Number XXXI.

[11] Percy A. Scholes, *The Oxford Companion to Music,* Tenth Edition, edited by John Owen Ward (London: Oxford University Press, 1970), p. 316.

[12] Published by E. C. Schirmer Music Co.

[13] "Constitution on the Sacred Liturgy," Article 14, 1963.

[14] John H. Snow, "The Future of the Church," a lecture delivered, p. 10.

[15] Saal quoting Messiaen.

[16] Quentin and Mary Margaret Faulkner, "Good Music is Good Prayer," *Liturgy*, Vol. 1, No. 4, p. 65.

Appendix I

Suggested Alternate Tunes:

4	Rejoice, rejoice, believers	Llangloffan, No. 761
37	Gentle Mary laid her child	Tempus Adest Floridum, No. 136
46	Brightest and best of the sons of the morning	Star in the East, No. 762 a, b
63	The royal banners forward go	Spires, No. 61
66	Sing, my tongue, the glorious battle	Atonement, No. 764
87	Welcome, happy morning	King's Weston, No. 763
94	Come, ye faithful, raise the strain	Hatfield, No. 765
100	The Sabbath day was by	St. Michael, No. 113
108	O come, Creator Spirit, come	St. David, No. 766
112	When Christ was born in Bethlehem	St. Magnus, No. 106
116	O Sion, open wide thy gates	Winchester Old, No. 13 (First Tune)
120	Around the throne of God a band	Wareham, No. 119
125	Hark! the sound of holy voices	Hyfrydol, No. 347 (Second Tune)
127	How bright these glorious spirits shine	Land of Rest, No. 585 (First Tune)
135	Blessed feasts of blessed martyrs	Holy Manna, No. 767 a, b
151	Awake, my soul, and with the sun	Tallis' Canon, No. 165
152	All praise to thee, who safe hast kept	Tallis' Canon, No. 165
171	O Trinity of blessed light	Wareham, No. 119
173	O Brightness of the immortal Father's face	Evening Hymn, No. 768
191	Thou, who at thy first Eucharist didst pray	Song 1, No. 470
209	O saving Victim, opening wide	Spires, No. 61
213	Shepherd of souls, refresh and bless	Windsor, No. 284
215	Lord, who at Cana's wedding feast	Kingsfold, No. 101
216	May the grace of Christ our Saviour	Stuttgart, No. 1
227	All things are thine; no gift have we	Herr Jesu Christ, No. 159 (Second Tune)
258	Christ is the world's true light	Darmstadt, No. 14
265	Eternal God, whose power upholds	Forest Green, No. 21 (First Tune)
270	Holy, Holy, Holy Lord	Dix, No. 52
274	Ancient of Days, who sittest throned in glory	Lombard Street, No. 575
281	Joyful, joyful, we adore thee	Hymn to Joy, No. 769
290	Let all the world in ev'ry corner sing	MacDougall, No. 770
292	Songs of praise the angels sang	Northampton, No. 771
294	Sing, my soul, his wondrous love	Song 13, No. 451

Appendix II

A Suggested Use of Handbells

One simple way to use handbells on a plainsong chant (such as the *Benedictus es, Domine*) would be to assign four bells to play at the beginning and midpoint of the verse:

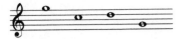

...and three bells to play on or after the final note of the chant.

The bells could be played at the beginning and ending of the verses either as a chord, or separately, in a peal; or you could begin one verse in one way and the second verse in another. The bells might also sound for a verse in a continuous pattern:

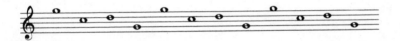

Appendix III

A Suggested List of Anthems for Small Choirs

Anthems for Unison Choir. G. Schirmer.

Bach, J. S. "Lord Jesus Christ, Thou Prince of Peace," unison with violin. Concordia.

Bach, J. S. "O Sacred Head, Now Wounded," with flute. Concordia.

Bach, J. S. "At Thy Feet." Mills Music Inc.

Billings, William. "When Jesus Wept." Mercury.

Buxtehude, Dietrich. "God Shall Do My Advising." Concordia.

Buxtehude, Dietrich. *In dulci jubilo*, with flutes and violins. Concordia.

Buxtehude, Dietrich. "Lord, Keep Us Steadfast in Thy Word," with two violins. Concordia.

Christiansen, Paul. "That Easter Morning." Augsburg.

Felciano, Richard. "Cosmic Festival." E. C. Schirmer.

Felciano, Richard. "The Eyes of All Hope in Thee." E. C. Schirmer.

Franck, Melchior. "Father, Thy Holy Spirit Send." E. C. Schirmer.

Hammerschmidt, Andreas. "Let the People Praise Thee." Concordia.

Handel, G. F. "Jesus, Sun of Life, My Splendour." Concordia.

Harrison, Frank L. *Now Make We Merthe* I, II, III. Oxford.

Howells, Herbert. "Mine Eyes for Beauty Pine." Oxford.

Lotti, Antonio. "Sing Joyous Christians." Concordia.

Lotti, Antonio, "Surely He Hath Borne Our Griefs." E. C. Schirmer.

Moe, Daniel. "I Lift Up Mine Eyes." Mercury.

Mozart, W. A. *De Profundis*, K. 93. Kalmus.

Near, Gerald. "He whom Joyous Shepherds." Calvary Press.

Powell, Robert J. "From the Rising of the Sun." Abingdon.

Powell, Robert J. "Jesus, Name of Wondrous Love." Abingdon.

Proulx, Richard. "My Heart is Full Today." Augsburg.

Proulx, Richard. "Of the Kindness of the Lord." Augsburg.

Rorem, Ned. "Sing, My Soul, His Wondrous Love." Peters.

Rorem, Ned. "Love Divine, All Loves Excelling." Peters.

Rutter, John. "Thy Perfect Love." Oxford.

Scheidt-Nelson. "Good Christians, Now Rejoice." Augsburg.

Schroeder, Hermann. "A Dove Flew Down." Concordia.

Schroeder, Hermann. "In Bethlehem a Wonder." Concordia.

Schroeder, Hermann. "Let Our Gladness Know No End." Concordia.

Schroeder, Hermann. "Wake Shepherds, Wake." Concordia.

Schütz, Heinrich. *Four Psalms*. Mercury.

Suitor, M. Lee. "Here, O My Lord." Agape.

Terry, R. R. "Richard de Castre's Prayer to Jesus." G. Schirmer.

Vulpius, Melchior. "Today is Christ Risen," with brass. Concordia.

White, Louis. *Gloria in excelsis*. Concordia.

Willan, Healey. "O Sacred Feast." H. W. Gray.

Williamson, Malcolm. "I Will Lift Up Mine Eyes." Boosey and Hawkes.

Williamson, Malcolm. "O Jerusalem." Boosey and Hawkes.

Williamson, Malcolm. *Six Wesley Songs*. Weinberger.

Williamson, Malcolm. *Six Christmas Songs*. G. Schirmer.

Williamson, Malcolm. "The King of Love." Boosey and Hawkes.

Williamson, Malcolm. "Together in Unity." Boosey and Hawkes.

Williamson, Malcolm. "Who is the King of Glory?" Boosey and Hawkes.

Wills, Arthur. *Three Popular Psalms*. G. Schirmer.

Wyton, Alec. "Stephen." Harold Flammer.

Wyton, Alec. "Transfiguration." Harold Flammer.

— NOTES —

— NOTES —